Margie Ralph is a great catechist! Her ability to explain complex ideas in clear, logical, and straightforward ways is unmatched. Not only will you learn a great deal about Scripture, but you will also have extraordinary teaching skills modeled before your very eyes!

  Leif Kehrwald, *General Editor,* **The Catholic Faith** *& Family Bible and currently Training Services Coordinator for* **Vibrant Faith**, *an ecumenical Christian ministry development group*

Ralph writes with exquisite clarity and wisdom, all the while deftly helping the reader understand how the Scriptures are best interpreted and explained within their original contexts. Although written for catechists, this jewel of a book has much to offer anyone who desires a better foundational grasp of our sacred texts.

  Neil A Parent, *author of* **A Concise Guide to Adult Faith Formation** *and former Executive Director of NCCL*

We have many excellent "what" books that explore the content of the Bible and its many books. Margie Ralph has written a "how" book that presents Catholic approaches and tools to read, interpret, understand, and appreciate the Bible. And she provides practical direction for applying these insights and tools to our lives and to teaching Scripture today. Every catechist and catechetical leader will find her book an essential guide for making the Bible central to faith formation. Her chapter on the use and abuse of Scripture deserves careful reading by everyone!

  John Roberto, *President,* **LifelongFaith Associates** *and author of* **Reimagining Faith Formation for the 21st Century**

SCRIPTURE BASICS

The ESSENTIAL CATECHIST'S BOOKSHELF

Scripture Basics

a
CATECHIST'S GUIDE

Margaret Nutting Ralph

TWENTY
THIRD *23rd*
PUBLICATIONS
www.23rdpublications.com

TWENTY-THIRD PUBLICATIONS
1 Montauk Avenue, Suite 200, New London, CT 06320
(860) 437-3012 » (800) 321-0411 » www.23rdpublications.com

ISBN: 978-1-62785-147-3
Library of Congress Catalog Card Number: 2015957203
Printed in the U.S.A.

Contents

INTRODUCTION

Why write a book entitled *Scripture Basics* for catechists? After all, catechists are well-informed adult Catholics, motivated to share their faith and knowledge with their students. One might well presume that most catechists know and love Scripture and can share that knowledge and love with their students. However, forty years' experience teaching Scripture myself has taught me that many well-informed adult Catholics do not know what the Catholic Church teaches us about how to understand biblical passages.

This fact was illustrated dramatically several years ago when I was teaching Scripture to a class of adults. After teaching the Catholic approach to Scripture (to be explained soon), I asked if there were any comments or questions. A woman in the class raised her hand and said: "I was baptized Catholic as an infant. I went to Catholic grade school, high school, and college. I have worshipped in a Catholic Church my whole life. And, besides that, I am a nun, and I have never heard what you just taught."

I mention this because it may well be that you will find yourself in this same situation. By reading this book, you may be learning things about how to interpret Scripture that you have not previously been taught. Even if this is not your experience, it is still important for you, as a catechist, to understand that many adult Catholics have not been taught this information, because you will undoubtedly encounter such people among the parents of students in your religious education classes. It is very important that you be aware of, and responsive to, their situation.

This book addresses two main questions:

- What do catechists need to know about the Bible themselves in order to be able to teach Scripture to any age group?

- What do catechists need to do in order to teach Scripture effectively to others, especially to those who are not adults?

In the chapters in which I respond to the first question (What do we need to know?), I will try to model some important aspects of the answer to the second question (What do we need to do?). It is for this reason that five chapter titles begin with the word *teaching*: I am trying to model how to teach the subjects being discussed. After completing the chapters on what we need to know, we will address the question: What is age-appropriate catechesis when it comes to teaching Scripture? Information that is appropriate for adults is not always appropriate for children. Finally, we will reflect on catechetical methods, on essential components that contribute to teaching Scripture effectively.

Why is it of utmost importance that those of us who have the privilege and responsibility to teach Scripture are knowledgeable and competent? Because correctly understanding Scripture is core to our spiritual lives. Christians believe that Scripture—that is, the writings that appear in the Bible, in both the Old and New Testaments—contains God's word for God's people. For this reason, the Second Vatican Council declared that all Christians are to be "nourished and ruled" by Scripture (see *Dogmatic Constitution on Divine Revelation*, no. 21).

To be *nourished* by Scripture, we must receive the word into ourselves. That is why, as Catholics, we constantly seek to be fed not only at the table of the Eucharist but at the table of God's word. To be *ruled* by Scripture, we must embrace Scripture as having authority in our lives, and we must correctly understand what Scripture is teaching. To teach Scripture we must know what the Catholic Church teaches about the correct interpretation of biblical passages. This book is written to aid the catechist in all of these areas: to be nourished by Scripture, to be ruled by Scripture, and to be competent in echoing the good news that we have received to those whom we teach.

However, before we do anything else, we should begin our study with prayer. It is very important that your students see you as a person who personally believes in the good news being taught. The prayer with which I like to begin every class on Scripture is a traditional Roman Catholic prayer to the Holy Spirit:

> *Come, Holy Spirit.*
> *Fill the hearts of your faithful.*
> *Enkindle in us the fire of your love.*
> *Send forth your Spirit,*
> *and we shall be created,*
> *and you shall renew the face of the earth.*
> *Amen.*

In this prayer we freely acknowledge that we are involved in a process of being created. We are open to new knowledge, to new understandings, and we call upon the Holy Spirit to be with us and to inspire us as we seek a greater understanding of God's self-revelation to God's people.

Come, Holy Spirit, come.

The Bible *and the* Lectionary: Why Catechists Need *to* Know Both

I have often asked Catholics: "Are you familiar with the Bible?" Everyone responds with a firm "Yes!" However, after further conversation, I discover that their familiarity is not with the Bible, but with the Lectionary. They know what the Bible is, but they have never read the Bible. They think their knowledge of Lectionary readings is knowledge of the Bible. To teach Scripture, a catechist must be knowledgeable not only about the Lectionary but about the Bible. Therefore, in this chapter we will address three questions:

- What is the Bible?

- What is the Lectionary?

- Why must a catechist be familiar with both the Bible and the Lectionary?

WHAT IS THE BIBLE?

The word *bible* means *the books*. In other words, the Bible is a library with books, not a book with chapters. However, Christians believe that this collection of books is unique because it contains God's self-revelation to God's people. Therefore, if we want answers to theological questions, questions that concern God, God's nature, our relationship to God and to each other, as well as how to live a life pleasing to God, there is no greater source of wisdom on earth than the collection of books that we call the Bible. The Bible teaches us what we need to know for "the sake of our salvation" (*Dogmatic Constitution on Divine Revelation*, no. 11).

Christians also claim that, in a sense, God is the author of the Bible. However, this is not a claim that in some miraculous way God wrote the Bible and that we received it as a finished product. Nor is it a claim that God or an angel dictated the text to an individual person and we received the Bible from that person. Rather, Christians believe that the Bible is the end result of a five-step process that took place over a period of two thousand years. The five steps are: events, oral tradition, written tradition, edited tradition, and some traditions becoming canonical.

A FIVE-STEP PROCESS

The first step in the process is that God revealed God's self through events. The events that underlie the Bible started in about 1850 BC, the time of Abraham and Sarah, our ancestors in faith, and ended shortly after the first century AD with the Spirit-filled birth and growth of the early church.

The events that lie behind what we Christians call the *Old Testament* include:

- the chosen people originally settling in the Holy Land

- their exodus from slavery in Egypt some 600 years later (1250 BC)

- their return to the Holy Land where they eventually established a united kingdom under David around 1000 BC

- the split of that kingdom (922 BC), with the ten northern tribes eventually being conquered by the Assyrians (721 BC) and the two southern tribes being conquered by the Babylonians (587 BC)

- the Babylonian exile (587–537 BC)

- the return to the Holy Land, first under Persian rule, then Greek rule interrupted by a short time of self-rule, and finally Roman rule

The events that lie behind the New Testament include Jesus' birth, public ministry, crucifixion, death, resurrection, and post-resurrection appearances as well as the birth of the church and the spread of the church throughout the then-known world.

Stories intended to teach what the people had learned about God and their covenant relationship with God through these events were first passed on through oral tradition. The stories were told in a variety of literary forms: legends, birth narratives, parables, allegories, to name but a few (more about this in Chapter 2). The lessons learned were based on the people's experience of historical events, but the stories told were not trying to teach history. Rather, the stories were intended to teach what these events had revealed to the people about the ultimate questions in life, questions that are just as important for us as they were for our ancestors in faith: Does life have a purpose? Just who is God? What is our relationship to God? What is right living?

Over time, various oral accounts were written down. Different authors emphasized different parts of the stories in order to respond to the needs of their contemporary audiences. With the passage of time, authors combined stories or edited stories in the light of subsequent events, events that had caused them to have questions or to have additional insights about what previous stories had taught.

CANONICITY

The fifth step of the process that resulted in the Bible that we now have is that some of these works became canonical, became part of the Bible, and others did not. The root word for *canonical* means *ruler*, that by which we measure things. If a book is in the canon, that means that the church believes that the book contains revelation and that the authors were inspired.

The books in what we Christians call the *Old Testament* and what we call the *New Testament* became canonical through a process that involved the Spirit working in the community. The books of the Old Testament gradually became canonical after the Babylonian exile. When the people returned to the Holy Land and rebuilt their temple, they were living under Persian rule. They no longer had their king or kingdom. Therefore, their self-identity became focused on their covenant relationship with God (*covenant* and *testament* are synonyms) and on their life of worship in the second temple. The temple priests became their most influential leaders. Gradually, the law (the Torah, the first five books of the Old Testament), the prophets, and the writings became accepted as canonical books.

The New Testament books became canonical because the believing community embraced them and began to use them in their worship services when they gathered in each other's homes to celebrate Eucharist. The early church fathers would compare notes to share information about which books were nourishing the worshipping community and faithfully teaching the core beliefs of Christianity. By the end of the second century, the four gospels that we now have were in general use, and, by the end of the fourth century, nearly the whole New Testament was in general use. The official "closing of the canon" did not happen until the sixteenth century at the Council of Trent. During the Reformation, some reformers wanted to remove some of the books that had been used through the centuries. In response to this challenge, the Council of Trent declared that we would neither subtract from, nor add to, the canon as it had stood for 1500 years.

OLD TESTAMENT/NEW TESTAMENT

You may have noticed that I have, on occasion, used the phrases about what "we Christians call" the *Old Testament* or the *New Testament*. There are two reasons for my using this phrase. One is that for several hundred years there was no such thing as a New Testament that was separate from an Old Testament. A New Testament, as distinct from an Old Testament, did not exist, because the events surrounding Jesus Christ were understood to be a continuation of the same story. After all, Christians believe that Jesus Christ is the fulfillment of the law and the prophets. The second reason is that while all Christians have the same books in the New Testament, we do not all have the same books in the Old Testament. Each of these reasons needs further explanation.

THE NEW TESTAMENT

At the time of Jesus, the books of Scripture were not in codices, that is, in bound books. Rather, they were on scrolls. You will remember when Jesus was in the synagogue in Nazareth and read from the prophet Isaiah, he read from a scroll (Luke 4:17). A collection of scrolls does not have to be in a certain order. However, when codices, bound books, were invented, what had been individual scrolls were transcribed into a format that resulted in a larger whole, an overarching narrative based on the order of the scrolls included.

In the second century, codices that included transcriptions of the canonical scrolls also included Christian writings. There was no division into Old and New Testaments, simply a combining of the overall story in one large volume. It was not until the fourth and fifth centuries, when the Gentile Christian church became progressively detached from its Jewish roots, that Bibles distinguished between an Old and a New Testament. Nevertheless, the Christian Church continued to affirm both Testaments. The New Testament did not replace the Old Testament. Indeed, knowledge of the Old Testament is an essential part of understanding the New Testament.

DIFFERENCES IN THE OLD TESTAMENT CANON

While all Christians have a New Testament canon consisting of the same twenty-seven books, Christians do not all agree on the Old Testament canon. Catholics and Greek Orthodox accept some books as canonical that are not included in the Protestant Old Testament. The reason for this difference is not primarily doctrinal, but historical. At the time of Jesus' public ministry, there were two collections of books that were comparable to what Christians now call the *Old Testament*: one in Hebrew, and one in Greek. The Greek version, called the

Septuagint, included a translation of the Hebrew Scriptures as well as some additional books that developed during the Hellenistic period (the time when the Greeks ruled). These additional books, most of which were originally written in Greek, were not in the Hebrew Scriptures.

The early church used the Greek Scriptures. When Jerome translated the Bible into Latin, he included the books that were in the Septuagint, but not in the Hebrew Scriptures. Catholics have continued to include these books, but the Protestant reformers, who wanted to rely on the original Hebrew texts rather than on the Greek translations, did not include them.

The books in question are Tobit, Judith, Wisdom, Ecclesiasticus (Sirach), Baruch, and 1 and 2 Maccabees. To acknowledge that not all Christians accept the books, they are sometimes referred to as *deuterocanonical* books. They are also call *apocryphal* (not part of the canon) by those who do not accept them. However, even when the books are not acknowledged as part of the canon, they are held in deep respect. Often a Protestant Bible will include the Apocrypha along with the Old and New Testaments. This means that the disputed books appear in the text between the Old and New Testaments.

WHAT IS THE LECTIONARY?

The Lectionary is the book that contains the collection of readings that are proclaimed during the Liturgy of the Word when we celebrate Mass. The Lectionary takes biblical passages out of their biblical context and places them into the context of a celebration of the liturgical year. The present collection of readings exists because the Second Vatican Council's *Constitution on the Sacred Liturgy* (no. 51) teaches that the "treasures of the Bible are to be opened up more lavishly, so that a richer fare may be provided for the faithful at the table of God's word."

In response to this teaching, the Catholic Church developed a Sunday Lectionary that celebrates the liturgical year in a three-year cycle. In each year (A, B, C) of the cycle, the liturgical year has the same form:

- four weeks of the Advent season, preparing for the coming of Christ

- the Christmas season, beginning with the Christmas vigil and ending on the Sunday after the Epiphany with the Baptism of the Lord

- Ordinary Time, between the Baptism of the Lord and Lent

- Lent, which begins with Ash Wednesday and continues through six Sundays

- the Easter Triduum: beginning Holy Thursday evening and ending Easter Sunday evening.

- the Easter Season, beginning with the Easter Vigil and ending seven weeks later with the feast of Pentecost

- Ordinary Time: extending from the Monday after Pentecost to the First Sunday of Advent

However, each year of the cycle centers on a different gospel: Year A on Matthew, Year B on Mark, and Year C on Luke. This arrangement gives us somewhat continuous readings from these gospels, and so the "treasures of the Bible are opened up more lavishly" for those gathered for worship.

In addition to the gospel reading, most Sundays (outside of the Easter season) also have a reading from the Old Testament and a second reading from the New Testament, but from a book other than a gospel. However, the readings from the Old Testament are not semi-continuous from one book. Rather, they are selected because they have a thematic unity with the gospel. This is because the readings at Mass (the Liturgy of the Word) and our celebration of Eucharist are both part of a single act of worship centered on Christ and Christ's paschal mystery. The Old Testament readings are selected in order to help us understand Jesus as the fulfillment of salvation history.

The readings from some other parts of the New Testament, such as the letters, *are* often semi-continuous. They allow us to see how the paschal mystery was lived out in the early church, and provide us with a model to do the same.

WHY CATECHISTS MUST KNOW THE BIBLE AS WELL AS THE LECTIONARY

Because the Lectionary takes biblical passages out of their biblical context, and because the Catholic Church teaches us that we must consider context in order to understand meaning (to be explained in Chapter 2), it is absolutely essential that anyone who attempts to teach Scripture have knowledge of the Bible, not just knowledge of those out-of-context biblical passages that appear in the Lectionary. Why? Because without knowledge of context, biblical passages can easily be misunderstood and can be used to support ideas that no inspired biblical author ever taught (to be explained in Chapter 6).

Our worship setting is assuming that we have read the Bible and that we bring knowledge of context with us when we come to worship. Otherwise, we often cannot understand what is being proclaimed. Indeed, we cannot truly be nourished and ruled by Scripture—and help others be nourished and ruled as well—unless we have read and understood the Bible.

⚫ *Questions for Reflection or Discussion*

1. How would you respond to the question, "Are you familiar with the Bible?" What opportunities have you had to read various books of the Bible in their entirety? Why do you think the answer to this question is important?

2. Do you think the Bible contains revelation? What do you mean by the word *revelation*? What have you learned from the Bible that you consider revelatory? Why do human beings need revelation?

3. Do you believe that, in the past, God has revealed God's self through events? Do you think God still reveals God's self through events? In what ways has God revealed God's self to you?

4. Have you ever been puzzled by a reading you heard proclaimed from the Lectionary? If so, had you ever read the book in the Bible from which the passage was taken? Why might knowing the biblical context for the reading help you understand it?

Teaching How Catholics Are *to* Interpret Scripture: Consider Context

One hundred years ago, Catholics were not encouraged to read the Bible. At that time, the proper way to interpret biblical passages was greatly debated. Church leaders feared that private interpretation might lead to serious error. In fact, an *Admonition* often appeared in Catholic Bibles, such as the following, which appeared in a nineteenth-century edition of the Douay-Rheims Bible:

> To prevent and remedy this abuse [i.e. mistaking the true sense of Scripture], and to guard against error, it was judged necessary to forbid the reading of the Scriptures in the vulgar languages, without the advice and permission of the Pastors and spiritual Guides whom God has appointed to govern his Church...
>
> Nor is this due submission to the Catholic Church...to be understood of the ignorant and

unlearned only, but also of men accomplished in
all kinds of learning; the ignorant fall into errors
for want of knowledge, and the learned through
pride and self-sufficiency.

Now, Catholics are encouraged to read the Bible and are
taught how to understand what the original inspired authors
were teaching their audiences (to be discussed in this chapter).
Based on that knowledge, Catholics are also encouraged to
hear the words of the Bible as living words that can be a light
to our paths (to be discussed in Chapter 5). What happened
to bring about this change?

Many people think that Vatican II happened, and that
the change came in 1965 with the Vatican II document *Dei
Verbum* (*Dogmatic Constitution on Divine Revelation*). However,
Dei Verbum was affirming what had been taught in an earlier
document: Pope Pius XII's encyclical *Divino Afflante Spiritu*
(*Inspired by the Holy Spirit*), which was published in 1943.
Divino Afflante Spiritu is considered to be the magna carta of
Catholic biblical scholarship. The truths taught by *Divino
Afflante Spiritu* and *Dei Verbum* are also reaffirmed in the
Catechism of the Catholic Church (1994). So, there is no question
that the Catholic Church does teach what we will explain in
this chapter. However, a great many Catholics are unaware
of this information. Therefore, the person who teaches other
adults this method of interpreting Scripture is often met with
skepticism and resistance.

Before explaining what the church teaches us on this sub-
ject, I want to emphasize that what we are explaining in this
chapter is part of the answer to the question: What do catechists need to know about the Bible themselves in order to
be able to teach Scripture to any age group? Catechists themselves need to have an adult understanding of Scripture no

matter what the age of the children whom the catechists are teaching. However, it is also true that some of what an adult needs to know in order to teach children is not age appropriate to pass on to the children. We will explain why in Chapter 7.

CONSIDER THE CONTEXT

In a single word, the Catholic Church teaches us to be *contextualists.* A contextualist is a person who considers context in order to determine meaning. The word often used for a person who does not consider context in order to determine meaning is *fundamentalist.* When we use the words *contextualist* and *fundamentalist,* it is very important that we define them. Otherwise, we are very likely to be misunderstood.

The word *fundamentalist* has changed meaning over time. The word first referred to a person who centers in on the fundamentals of the faith. It has come to mean a person who takes a passage out of its biblical context and applies a meaning to the passage that has nothing to do with what the original inspired author was teaching. For instance, a fundamentalist might insist that God created the world and all that exists in six days. The fundamentalist would not think to ask, "Is the inspired author addressing the topic that I am using the passage to address?"

A fundamentalist often accuses a contextualist of not believing that biblical authors are inspired or not believing that the Bible contains revelation. However, the disagreement between fundamentalists and contextualists has nothing to do with these topics. Both believe that the authors are inspired and that the Bible teaches revelation. The only difference is that a contextualist believes that in order to correctly understand what the inspired author is teaching, we must consider the contexts in which the passage appears in the Bible. These contexts include the literary form in which the author is writing, the shared beliefs at the time of the author and his audience, and the fact that the Bible models a two-thousand-year process of coming to understand the truths about which it teaches. Each of these contexts needs further explanation.

Consider the Literary Form

In Chapter 1, we said that the Bible is a library of books, not a book with chapters. We also said that when people who had experienced God's power and presence in events wanted to teach what they had come to understand, they told stories, and that the stories were in many different literary forms. Over time the stories were collected and included in the library that we call the Bible.

We are all very familiar with the concept of literary form. We know that a school or town library contains mythologies, legends, song books, histories, biographies, encyclopedias, novels, works of science fiction, etc. If we read a myth or a novel and think it is history, we will misunderstand the intent of the author. When reading Scripture, to misunderstand the intent of the author is a big mistake, because Catholics are taught to put the authority of Scripture behind the intent of the author. As the *Catechism* says, "In Sacred Scripture, God speaks to man in a human way. To interpret Scripture correctly, the reader must be attentive to what the human authors truly wanted to affirm and to what God wanted to reveal to us by their words" (no. 109).

In other words, if we fail to consider literary form, we are in danger of misunderstanding the intent of the author. If we misunderstand the intent of the author, we also misunderstand the revelation.

Adults sometimes feel intimidated by the idea that they must consider literary form in order to understand what a biblical author is teaching. I have often been asked: "How can I tell one literary form from another? After all, I'm not an English major." In response to this comment, I try my best to build people's confidence that they already have the skills needed to determine one literary form from another. It is just that they may not have realized that they need to apply this ability to their reading of Scripture.

We all use our ability to distinguish among literary forms when we read a newspaper. If our questions relate to facts, such as who, what, when, and where, the front page of the newspaper should answer our questions. The function of a front-page article is to inform.

However, this does not remain true when we read the editorial page. The function of an editorial is not to inform, but to persuade. If, after reading an editorial, I think that I have an objective understanding of an issue, I will be wrong. It is not the author's fault that I have misunderstood. It is my own, because I misunderstood the kind of writing I was reading.

If I read a comic strip like *Doonesbury*, and one of the characters in the strip, such as Zonker, has a conversation with the president of the United States, I do not conclude that such a conversation actually took place, even though I read the words attributed to the president in a newspaper. I recognize that by picturing the conversation taking place between a fictional character and a historical character, the author is clearly telling me that he is not reporting an event.

There are many ways that authors inform readers about the literary form being used. We recognize these clues even if we do not know the names of the devices being used. For instance, if an author has an animal or a plant talk, just as if the animal or plant were a human being, he is not teaching history or claiming a miracle, but is using a literary device called *personification*. If an author pictures God as a moody, fallible human being, he is not describing a vision, but is composing an *anthropomorphic* picture of God, another literary device. So, in order to determine the kind of writing we are reading in the Bible, we need to bring the same common sense to our reading of the Bible that we bring to everything else that we read.

Consider the beliefs of the time

The *Catechism of the Catholic Church* reminds us that, in addition to literary form, we must consider the context of the beliefs of the time: "In order to discover *the sacred authors' intention,* the reader must take into account the conditions of their time and culture, the literary genres in use at that time, and the modes of feeling, speaking and narrating then current" (no. 110).

In the course of teaching the truth about the people's relationship with God—the topic that is the inspired author's reason for telling a story in the first place—the author may say something by way of example or application that reflects the beliefs of the time. We do not put the authority of Scripture behind examples or applications. We put the authority of Scripture behind the core truth that the author is teaching.

An example will make this point clear. Say that on a beautiful spring day I am overwhelmed by the beauty of creation. I experience it as a gift from God to all of God's beloved people, saint and sinner alike. I want to compose a story that will enable others to experience the beauty of nature in the same way. So, I begin my story by picturing God creating the world with love. Since I live in the twenty-first century and know that the earth is round, I will picture God creating a round earth. However, had I lived in 450 BC and had exactly the same experience and the same insight, I would have pictured God creating a flat earth that rests on four posts. That was the presumption of the time. Remember, the shape of the earth is irrelevant to the point I am trying to make—that God created the world in love. It is not my intention to teach anything about the shape of the earth. That is a scientific question. I am simply referring to the earth as being shaped the way I presume it is in the process of teaching something else entirely.

History has taught us that when we fail to consider the beliefs of the time, we are in danger of using Scripture to support our own prejudices, thus inadvertently treating unjustly other beloved children of God. We will give examples of this danger in Chapter 6, when we discuss the use and abuse of Scripture.

Consider the two-thousand-year process of revelation

The third context that we must consider in order to correctly interpret Scripture is the context of the two-thousand-year period that it took Scripture to reach its present form. The Bible is not comparable to a catechism that gives bottom-line doctrinal responses to our questions. Rather, the Bible probes mystery through narrative. The people who are telling the stories, who are sharing what they have learned through their experiences, model a process of coming to deeper and deeper understandings.

This means that another mistake that we can make when reading the Bible is to take an early insight and think that it is the whole truth, or to take an early insight and contrast it to a later insight as though the two are contradictory rather than being steps in a process of coming to a deeper and deeper understanding.

For instance, in Exodus we read: "You shall give life for life, eye for eye, tooth for tooth, hand for hand, foot for foot, burn for burn, wound for wound, stripe for stripe" (Ex 21:23–25). However, Jesus teaches that "if anyone strikes you on the right cheek, turn the other also; and if anyone wants to sue you and take your coat, give your cloak as well; and if anyone forces you to go one mile, go also the second mile" (Matt 5:39–41). Is Jesus contradicting Exodus?

Actually, Jesus is standing on the shoulders of his ancestors in the faith and is building on Exodus. That is why Jesus says, "Do not think that I have come to abolish the law or the prophets; I have come not to abolish but to fulfill" (Matt 5:17).

The "eye for an eye and tooth for a tooth" quotation is teaching against revenge. It is teaching a proportioned response: people should not do worse to their enemies than their enemies have done to them. This teaching dates to the time of the exodus, about 1250 BC. It is a step forward in understanding the ramifications of the fact that God is love. However, this teaching does not represent the fullness of understanding that God's beloved people came to over time.

Jesus' teaching takes us even further. After instructing the crowds to turn the other cheek, he continues: "You have heard that it was said, 'You shall love your neighbor and hate your enemy.' But I say to you, Love your enemies and pray for those who persecute you, so that you may be children of your Father in heaven..." (Matt 5:43–45a). We are to love our enemies so that they may have a concrete witness of God's love for them. While this is a depth of understanding we did not have earlier, it is still not contradicting earlier teachings. To contradict would be to say, "Destroy your enemy!" Truly, Jesus does fulfill—make fuller—the law and the prophets.

None of us wants to inadvertently abuse Scripture. We want to be faithful witnesses of God's love for God's people. In order to avoid abusing Scripture, we must actually read the Bible, and we must read the Bible as contextualists. Only then will we be able to understand God's revelation to God's people, the revelation that is proclaimed in all of our worship settings.

✸ *Questions for Reflection or Discussion*

1. Up to this point, would you describe yourself as a contextualist or as a fundamentalist? Why does the Catholic Church teach us to be contextualists?

2. When you read the newspaper, do you distinguish among literary forms? What "permissions" do you give various authors (a front-page journalist, an editorialist, a comic-strip writer)? Have you applied this ability to your reading of Scripture? Explain your response.

3. Why do we put the authority of Scripture behind the intent of the author rather than behind what the author says by way of example or application? Do you think this distinction has any relevance today? Explain your response.

4. Why is it dangerous to understand a partial truth and think it is the whole truth? Do you think this distinction has any relevance today? Explain your response.

Teaching *an* Old Testament Application

In this chapter, in which we apply what we have learned about considering context to a passage from the Old Testament, we are still responding to the question: What do catechists need to know about the Bible themselves in order to be able to teach Scripture to any age group? At the same time, we must remember that not everything discussed in this chapter is appropriate content to teach to anyone younger than a junior in high school. The reasons for this statement will be explained in Chapter 7, when we discuss age-appropriate catechesis. You might well be asking: If catechists should not teach all of this information to children, why do catechists, themselves, need to know it? This question, too, will be addressed in Chapter 7.

AN APPLICATION TO THE STORY OF THE MAN AND WOMAN IN THE GARDEN

The second story in the first book in the library of books that we call the Bible is the story of the man and woman in the garden. Before teaching an application of our contextualist method of interpretation to the story, it is very important that we read the story (Gen 2:4—3:24). We want to give the inspired author the first voice, and the authoritative voice, in teaching us the eternal truths that are being taught through the story.

After reading this second story, it becomes immediately evident that it is not a continuation of the previous one. By the time the first story ended, the story of God creating the world in six days, everything had been created, including human beings, both male and female. As this story begins, human beings do not yet exist. The reason that this obvious seam in the collected materials is there is that the story of creation was added as a preface to already existing material during the last editing stage after the Babylonian exile. We are now reading a separate story with a different topic.

Consider the literary form

The author gives us many clues as to his literary form. For instance, the author uses *personification*. That is, he has something that is not human behave as though it were human: one of the characters in the story is a talking snake. That alone tells us that we are not reading history and that the author is not teaching anything of a scientific nature.

The author also uses many other symbols. The man and woman do not eat the forbidden fruit of an apple tree, but the forbidden fruit of the tree of the knowledge of good and evil. There is also a tree of life, another obvious symbol. Still another symbol is not obvious in the English translation. In English, *Adam* sounds like a masculine, singular noun. However, in Hebrew, the language in which this story was originally written, *adam* is a neuter, collective noun. It refers to humankind. So, the story is about each of us. We are each *Adam*.

Still another clue to the literary form of the story is that God is pictured as though God were a human being. This is called an *anthropomorphic* picture of God. God is not all-knowing. God has to experiment in order to find a suitable partner for the human. God does not know that the man and woman have eaten the forbidden fruit until they hide from God and God asks why they are hiding.

So, it is evident that we are reading an imaginative and symbolic story. God is a character in the story. The story is probing a mystery beyond our comprehension (to be explained). The name of the literary form of such a story is *myth*.

However, if, when we teach the literary form of the story, we use the word *myth,* we must be very careful to define what we mean by the word. If we don't define the word, people will misunderstand us to be saying that the story is not true. That is because the word *myth*, in English, is a homonym: the word *myth*, spelled the same and pronounced the same, has two completely different meanings. *Myth* can mean the name of a literary form that teaches profound truths, or it can mean something once believed to be true but now known to be false. The second meaning is the one most often used. However, that is not the word we are using. We are using the word *myth* to name a literary form that probes mystery through symbolic language and that teaches us something about our relationship with God.

As is true of every literary form, a myth can be a vehicle to teach truth, or a myth can teach something false. To name the literary form is not to comment on the truth or falsity of what the story teaches. For example, in a letter (a literary form), I can tell you the truth, or I can tell you a lie. Either way, the literary form is still a letter. Just so, a myth could teach something true about our relationship with God, or it could teach something false. The fact that this myth appears in the canon means that the believing community found that this myth teaches something true, something that every generation needs to hear.

So, our next questions are: What is this story about? What mystery is it probing, and what is it teaching? Many people refer to this story as the second story of creation. However, creation is only an early plot element in the story. The mystery of creation doesn't begin to describe the whole plot. An accurate plot summary is: There is a place of no suffering. Humankind chooses to act contrary to God's revealed moral order. There is a place of suffering. This story is responding to the question: Why do human beings suffer?

What is the story teaching?

The story of the man and woman in the garden is teaching that sin causes suffering. Let us look at the plot and see how, through symbolic language, the author teaches this profound insight about our relationship with God.

The story begins with God creating *adam*, the human being. God knows that it is not good for a human being to be alone, so God creates the other person whom we all need: someone whom we can know and love, and who can know and love us.

The human beings know what is right and what is wrong because God has told Adam, "You may freely eat of every tree of the garden; but of the tree of the knowledge of good and evil you shall not eat, for in the day that you eat of it you shall die" (Gen 2:16–17). In other words, God reveals to human beings that there is a moral order built into creation. If human beings act contrary to this moral order, they will immediately bring death upon themselves. This line is very important because it tells us that the story is about spiritual life and death, not physical life and death. On the day that the man and woman eat the forbidden fruit, they do not die physically, but they do die spiritually.

Before the act of disobedience, the man and woman are not

28

suffering. They are free of suffering because all of their relationships are in right order: their relationship with self, other, God, and the earth. The man and woman's self-acceptance is symbolized by the fact that they are both naked, but they are not at all ashamed of who they are. They are so close to each other, they are like one person: the man says, "This at last is bone of my bones and flesh of my flesh" (Gen 2:23). They are in right relationship with God: God comes for a walk and a talk in the evenings. Finally, they are in right relationship with the earth: what they need is available to them.

All of these relationships are shattered when the woman and man freely choose to act contrary to the revealed moral order. Eating is a wonderful symbol for sinning, because eating is something we each choose to do, and what we eat becomes a part of us. Before eating the fruit of the forbidden tree, the man and woman have no knowledge of evil. They have known only good. Now, however, they have knowledge of both good and evil, and that changes everything.

The man and woman are still naked, but now they are ashamed of themselves. Instead of being in right relationship with each other and their world, they blame others: the man blames the woman and the woman blames the serpent. Instead of being in right relationship with God, they hide from God. Instead of being in right relationship with their environment, they will now suffer just to meet their daily needs. All of this suffering is the consequence of sin.

The kinds of suffering that the man and woman will experience are the kinds of suffering that the human race has known from experience throughout the centuries. For example, women will bear their children in pain. They will not be treated as beloved partners in marriage, but their husbands will "rule over" them (Gen 3:16). This description, placed on God's lips, is not God establishing God's social order. This is the author teaching that a husband's ruling over his wife is the fruit of sin, not the fruit of love. People will also suffer because they will have to work by the sweat of their brow to have food. Finally, human beings will suffer death. They will not be able to eat from the tree of life and live forever.

Notice that the author pictures God still loving the man and woman, even after they have sinned. God explains to them the consequences of their actions. God feels so sorry for them that "God made garments of skins for the man and for his wife, and clothed them" (Gen 3:21). It is not that God is punishing the man and woman by making them suffer. Rather, it is that the man and woman have brought suffering on themselves, suffering they could have avoided, if only they had not chosen to do the very thing that they knew was wrong. The story is teaching that sin inevitably causes suffering.

Consider the beliefs of the time

Scripture scholars believe that this story dates to about 1000 BC. The story is a perfect example of the importance of considering the second and third contexts that we are applying to our interpretation of Scripture: the beliefs of the time and the process of revelation. This story teaches something true, but it is a partial truth. Over time, more was understood, additional truths that did not deny the earlier insight, but added to it.

It is true that sin inevitably causes suffering. There is a moral order. God has revealed the moral order (Moses and the promulgation of the ten commandments date to about 1250 BC). To choose sin is to shatter one's relationships, not because God punishes sin, but because sin changes who we are. It destroys our integrity and our ability to be in right relationships. Instead of responding to God's love, we hide because we know what we have done. Instead of loving each other, we blame and find fault with each other. Instead of being good stewards of the earth, we pollute our environment. We have eaten the fruit of the tree of the knowledge of good and evil. The story of the man and woman in the garden teaches these eternal truths, and every generation needs to hear them.

However, while the insight "sin inevitably causes suffering" is true, is that insight the whole answer to the question, "Why do human beings suffer?" For centuries people believed that the answer to that question was "yes." However, the Israelites grew in their understanding of the mystery of suffering from the experience of the Babylonian exile. Works written in the light of the exile, such as 2 Isaiah (Isaiah 40 – 55) and the Book of Job, offer additional insights in response to questions about the reasons and purpose for human suffering.

Of course, the New Testament adds a great deal more to our understanding of the mystery of suffering. Jesus is an innocent person who suffers. Why did Jesus have to suffer? What was accomplished through Jesus' suffering? The New Testament explores these questions at length, often finding in the inspired words of the prophets the concepts and insights that enabled the early church to come to terms with the mystery of a crucified Messiah.

We see, then, that when we apply the contextualist method of interpretation to the story of the man and woman in the garden, we find that the author is teaching a universal truth. There is a moral order built into creation. That moral order has been revealed to us. When we act contrary to that moral order, when we sin, we inevitably bring suffering onto ourselves and others. This suffering has nothing to do with getting caught. It has to do with our personal integrity and our ability to love. To choose sin is never a wise choice.

 ## Questions for Reflection or Discussion

1. Is this contextualist interpretation of the story of the man and woman in the garden new to you? Do you agree that the author is not teaching history or science? What clues does the author give us about his literary form?

2. Do you agree that there is a moral order built in to creation and that sin inevitably causes suffering? Do you think our society generally agrees with these ideas? Explain your responses.

3. Do you think that any literary form can be a vehicle for truth? Explain your response. What stories did you read as a child that didn't teach history or science, but did teach truth?

4. Do you believe that innocent people suffer? Do you think that suffering has a purpose other than punishment for sin? What do you think that purpose might be? Are your responses based on observation? On reason? On personal experience? Explain your responses.

Teaching *a*
New Testament
Application

In our last chapter we applied the contextualist method of interpretation to a very well-known story from the Old Testament: the story of the man and woman in the garden. We saw that applying this method of interpretation to the biblical passage allowed us to discover the universal truth that the inspired author intended to teach, a truth that is just as important in the twenty-first century as it was in the century in which the story was originally written.

In this chapter we will demonstrate the richness of the contextualist method of interpretation by applying it to several New Testament parables. Once more, we will explain what a catechist needs to know in order to teach Scripture. We will leave the discussion of age-appropriate catechesis, that is, what of this adult understanding can be taught to children, until Chapter 7.

I have chosen to discuss parables because lack of knowledge about the literary form and the function of parables can lead to serious misinterpretations. People, including children,

who misinterpret parables often come away with a very negative image of God. To help students, as well as their parents,
avoid this mistake, it is crucial that catechists have an adult
understanding of the parables.

PARABLES

The parables that Jesus tells in the gospel are extremely well-
known. If I ask a group of Catholics if they know the parable
of the prodigal son, all nod their heads yes. I can substitute
almost any parable in the question—the parable of the good
Samaritan, the parable of the vineyard workers, the parable of
the talents, the parable of the wedding feast—and the answer
will still be yes. However, the reason Catholics know these
parables is often because they have heard them proclaimed at
Mass. That means their knowledge is from the Lectionary, not
from the Bible. They have often never read the parables in the
contexts in which they appear in the gospels.

So, if I ask the same group if they know to whom Jesus told
the parable of the prodigal son, or any other well-known parable, nearly all shake their heads no. Why does this matter? It
matters because the parables are the middle of a conversation
that Jesus is having with someone. The parable is addressed
to a specific person or group to call that person or group to
self-knowledge and conversion. If we don't know the social
context in which the parable is told, we often miss the lesson
that Jesus is teaching his audience and that the gospel author
is teaching his readers. Once more, in order to correctly interpret an inspired author's intent we must consider context. If
we miss the inspired author's intent, we miss the revelation.

PARABLES VERSUS ALLEGORIES

People who know a parable but do not know the context in
which the parable is told often unconsciously treat a parable as

though it were an allegory. It is this mistake that results in people forming a negative concept of God. To demonstrate this most important distinction, I will first explain the difference between a parable and an allegory. I will then demonstrate how not knowing the difference can lead to harmful error.

The lesson of a parable is derived from a single comparison between someone or something in the story and the audience to whom Jesus tells the story. Through that comparison, Jesus is teaching the listeners something about themselves, something to which they may be blind, or something that they are reluctant to see or admit. Through the parable, Jesus is teaching his listeners something pertinent to their spiritual lives, something they really need to hear.

In contrast, the lesson of an allegory is derived, not from a **single** comparison between the audience and someone in the story, but from **a series of comparisons** between two levels of meaning in the story: the literal level and the implied level. The plot elements on the literal level stand for something on the implied level. To interpret an allegory, we do not need to know the audience to whom it is told. All we need to do is understand the series of comparisons between the literal and implied levels of meaning.

Because those of us familiar with the Lectionary readings hear parables out of their biblical context, we often interpret the parables as though they were allegories, not realizing that this is what we are doing. It is not always wrong to do this. In fact, the early church interpreted parables as allegories, and some of the allegorical interpretations appear in the gospel. An example is Jesus' parable of the sower (see Mark 4:3–8 for the parable and Mark 4:13–20 for the allegorical interpretation).

If it is not always wrong to allegorize a parable, why is it important that we know the difference between an allegory and a parable? The reason is that while interpreting a parable as though it were an allegory does not always lead to error, on occasion it does lead to serious error. An example of interpreting a parable as though it were an allegory when it causes no harm, and an example when it causes great harm, will make the point clear.

An example where no harm is caused

We all know the parable of the prodigal son (Luke 15:11–32). I have often heard this parable read when we are celebrating the sacrament of reconciliation. In that setting, the homilist interprets the parable as though it were an allegory, drawing a series of comparisons between the literal level of the story and the intended level: The father stands for God. The prodigal son stands for sinners like ourselves. The lesson is that God always welcomes back the sinner. Since God always does welcome back the sinner, the lesson drawn is compatible with Scripture. This is true even though the homilist has interpreted the parable as though it were an allegory and has used the parable to teach a different lesson than Luke is teaching when he includes this parable.

To understand what Luke is teaching, we must ask: To whom is Jesus speaking? What are Jesus and that person or persons talking about? How does the audience compare to someone or something in the story? What lesson, drawn from that comparison, is Jesus teaching the audience that is a personal call to conversion?

Jesus tells this parable to the Pharisees and scribes who "were grumbling and saying, 'This fellow welcomes sinners and eats with them'" (Luke 15:2). Jesus' critics compare to the older brother in the story. Through this single comparison, Jesus is teaching the Pharisees and scribes that they, like the older brother, are self-righteous and judgmental. They consid-

er themselves better than "sinners." They do not realize that
their inability to love the repentant sinner is, in itself, a sin

In Luke's gospel, through the parable of the prodigal son,
Jesus is calling the Pharisees and scribes to self-knowledge
and conversion. Jesus is teaching them something about
themselves to which they are blind, something they don't
want to hear.

So, the parable of the prodigal son can be used to teach
something true when interpreted as a parable in the context
of Luke's gospel (to judge others as sinners and exclude them
is itself a sin), and when interpreted as an allegory in the context of a penance service (God loves and forgives sinners).
Both messages are faithful to Scripture as a whole. However,
this is not the case when many other parables are allegorized.
If we interpret some parables as allegories, we find ourselves
teaching something contrary to Scripture as a whole.

A harmful allegorical interpretation

Another well-known parable is the parable of the talents
(Matt 25:14–30). I know of an occasion on which this parable
was used at a prayer service when children were being given
their report cards. The intent of the person reflecting on the
parable was to teach children that they shouldn't waste their
God-given abilities, a true and important lesson. However,
in selecting this scriptural passage to teach the message, he
allegorized a parable that does not lend itself to allegory and,
without meaning to do so, taught the children a very negative image of God. To see how this happened, and why it is a
harmful mistake, we will interpret the parable as an allegory.
We will then interpret the parable as a parable so that we
can see what the gospel author intended to teach through
the parable.

The allegorical interpretation of the parable of the talents

The person giving out report cards allegorized the parable, saying that the master in the story stands for God, the servants stand for the students, and the talents stand for the students' God-given abilities. Just as the master entrusted his servants with the talents, so has God entrusted the students with many gifts. Just as the master rewarded and punished his servants, so will God reward and punish the students, depending on whether or not they make good use of the gifts God has given them.

This is a very harmful interpretation of the parable of the talents because it teaches a very negative image of God. The master in this story does not stand for God. In fact, he is a very mean person, a person to justly fear. The original audience would never have thought of this master as standing for God, because he is an obvious sinner: he thinks his servant should have invested the money at interest. To invest money at interest, thereby gouging the poor, was a very sinful thing to do. The master has a reputation for being a harsh man, reaping where he does not sow. No wonder the servant is afraid of him. The master doesn't care about the servant at all, only about his profit. He has his servant thrown out in the "darkness, where there will be weeping and gnashing of teeth" (Matt 25:30). This master is exactly the opposite of the loving God whom Jesus Christ has revealed to us.

The parable of the talents interpreted as a parable

In order to understand what Matthew is using the parable to teach, we must interpret the story as a parable, not as an allegory. That is, we must put it in the context in which it appears in Matthew's gospel.

This parable is part of the long eschatological (i.e., about the end times) discourse that Jesus gives in answer to the disciples' question, "Tell us, when will this be, and what will be the sign of your coming and of the end of the age?" (Matt 24:3). So, the audience is the disciples and the topic is the end times.

Matthew's gospel was written about 80 AD. Jesus was expected to return on the clouds of heaven during the lifetime of Jesus' contemporaries. By the time Matthew is writing, the first-generation church is coming to terms with the fact that the second coming won't be as soon as expected. Matthew pictures Jesus telling two parables that address this time of waiting. One is the parable of the ten bridesmaids. This parable is teaching the disciples that, since they do not know when the Lord will come, they should be ready always. The second parable is the parable of the talents. Through this parable, Jesus is teaching his disciples that, as they wait for the coming of the Lord, they should not, out of fear, refuse to act.

The lesson of the parable is drawn from the single comparison between the disciples who are expecting the Lord to return and the servants who are expecting their master to return. During this time the disciples should do what they are called to do without fear. The reason the servant who failed did fail was because he let fear paralyze him: "I was afraid, and so I went and hid your talent in the ground" (Matt 25:25). Jesus' disciples are not to live in fear. This message is taught over and over in the gospels. Matthew, himself, has already taught it when he pictured Jesus sending the apostles on their mission (see Matt 10:16–31), and concluding with the comforting words: "So do not be afraid; you are of more value than many sparrows" (Matt 10:31).

So, we see that if we allegorize the parable of the talents, we inadvertently teach error: God is a mean master. If we interpret the parable as a parable, we teach what Matthew was using the parable to teach: we should not, out of fear, refuse to act. Once more, we put the authority of Scripture behind the intent of the author. Once more we find that we discover a universal truth, one that is just as applicable to us as it was to Matthew's original audience. We too are not to live in fear. Why? Because we are beloved of God.

Parables are valuable teaching tools. Scripture scholars think that when we read the parables we are getting the closest we can get to Jesus' actual words and style of teaching. The parables, in their social contexts, are teaching specific truths to specific people. When taken out of that context they can legitimately be used to teach additional lessons, but only if those lessons are compatible with Scripture as a whole. One way we catechists can avoid misinterpreting parables is to be consciously aware of the difference between a parable and an allegory. We don't want to teach our students, no matter what their age, that God is like some of the mean masters in the parables.

CONTEXT, CONTEXT, CONTEXT

We see, then, that it is just as important to consider context when interpreting New Testament stories as it is when interpreting Old Testament stories. If we fail to consider literary form, the beliefs of the time, and the process of revelation, we are likely to interpret parables in such a way that God appears as a mean master to be feared. The lesson that the inspired author intended to teach, "Do not be afraid," simply gets lost. As catechists who echo the good news of Jesus Christ to every generation, we want to be sure that when we teach Scripture, we teach what the inspired authors intended to teach, that is, what God wants us to know for the sake of our salvation.

✸ *Questions for Reflection or Discussion*

1. If someone asked you to describe God in just a
   few sentences, what would you say? On what do
   you base your concept of God? On Scripture? On
   experience? On doctrine? Explain your responses.

2. Are you familiar with the parables? Do you know to whom
   Jesus was speaking when he told various parables? Have
   any parables always puzzled you? Does the method of
   parable interpretation discussed in this chapter help you to
   better understand the parables? Explain your responses.

3. Why do you think Jesus used parables to call people
   to self-knowledge and conversion? What advantage
   does telling a parable have over direct criticism?

4. When you read a parable, do you ever side with the people
   who are being corrected, such as the all-day workers in the
   parable of the vineyard workers (Matt 20:1–16) or the older
   brother in the parable of the prodigal son (Luke 5:11–32)? What
   do you think this reaction might teach you about yourself?

Teaching Scripture *as a* Living Word

In our previous chapters, we have taught what the Catholic Church teaches about how to understand the revelation that Scripture contains: we must seek to understand the intent of the original inspired author by putting that author's words in the contexts in which they appear in the Bible. Those contexts include the chosen literary form, the shared beliefs of the author and the original audience, and the process of revelation that is apparent in the overarching narrative of the Bible. All of these teachings are correct, and they are very important. However, they do not represent the whole truth. It is also true that Scripture is a living word.

Scripture, itself, claims to be a living word. In the Letter to the Hebrews we read: "Indeed, the word of God is living and active, sharper than any two-edged sword, piercing until it divides soul from spirit, joints from marrow; it is able to judge the thoughts and intentions of the heart" (Heb 4:12).

In 2 Timothy we read: "But as for you, continue in what you have learned and firmly believed, knowing from whom you learned it, and how from childhood you have known the sacred writings that are able to instruct you for salvation through faith in Christ Jesus. All scripture is inspired by God and is useful for teaching, for reproof, for correction, and for training in righteousness, so that everyone who belongs to God may be proficient, equipped for every good work" (2 Tim 3:14–17). We express our belief in Scripture as a living word when we sing, "Your word is a lamp to my feet/and a light to my path" (Ps 119:105).

So, we have two claims that, at first glance, appear to contradict each other: on the one hand we say that to understand the revelation that is in Scripture we must consider context, and on the other hand we say that Scripture is a living word that can speak to the church of every generation and to each of us in the context of our lives. How can both of these assertions be true? In response to this question we will first explain what we mean by saying that Scripture is a living word. We will then explain how the two claims are compatible.

SCRIPTURE AS A LIVING WORD IN THE EARLY CHURCH

Scripture itself models the fact that the meaning of the words of Scripture are not exhausted by the intent of the original author. For example, the early church found in the words of the prophets meanings in addition to those meanings that the prophets themselves intended to teach. The suffering servant songs of Second Isaiah (Is 40 — 55) illustrate this point.

The prophet whose prophesies we hear in Second Isaiah was addressing the Israelites who were in exile in Babylon. This was a time of terrible suffering for the Israelites, not just because they were in exile, but because this experience was causing them to doubt their very self-identity as people living in a covenant relationship with God. The Israelites had understood their nation, their king, and their temple to be the outward signs of this covenant relationship. Now that the Babylonians had conquered them, they no longer had their own king and nation, their temple was destroyed, and they were living in a country that was not their own. This whole terrible experience caused them to ask: Are we still God's people? Is God still our God?

Second Isaiah begins by assuring the exiles that they are still God's people and God is still their God with the words, "Comfort, O comfort **my** people, says **your** God (Is 40:1 [emphasis added]). Second Isaiah then goes on to offer the people hope that their suffering is not punishment. Rather, God is doing something wonderful and new through them. Through the Israelites, all nations will come to know the Israelites' God. The Lord says, "I will give you as a light to the nations,/ that my salvation may reach to the end of the earth" (Is 49:6b).

In teaching this lesson, Second Isaiah personifies the Israelites in exile as God's suffering servant through whom all nations will come to know their God. In one suffering servant song, Second Isaiah pictures the kings of other nations saying, "But he was wounded for our transgressions,/crushed for our iniquities;/upon him was the punishment that made us whole,/and by his bruises we are healed" (Is 53:5).

When Jesus was alive, the Jews expected a messiah who would free them from Roman rule. They did not expect a messiah who would be crucified by the Romans. Jesus' death was a terribly painful mystery to his followers, a mystery that dashed the hopes they had placed in him. No one had understood the words of the prophets as predicting a crucified messiah. The cross was not only a mystery but a scandal.

However, in the light of the crucifixion and post-resurrection appearances, and in their terrible need to make sense of it all, those in the first-generation church found in the words of the prophets the mental concepts and the words they needed to begin to understand and to preach what they had come to understand, based on their experiences. They now understood Jesus to be God's suffering servant. They now understood that Jesus was God's self-revelation to the whole world. Without denying Second Isaiah's original intent, the prophet's words took on a second level of meaning, a meaning that the church believed God had intended all along.

That the early church began to see additional meanings in the words of the prophets is evident in Luke's story of the two disciples on the road to Emmaus (see Luke 24:13–35). As the story begins, the disciples are completely dejected because Jesus has been crucified. When Jesus joins them, they do not recognize him. On hearing why they are so sad, Jesus says, "'Oh, how foolish you are, and how slow of heart to believe all that the prophets have declared! Was it not necessary that the Messiah should suffer these things and then enter into his glory?' Then beginning with Moses and all the prophets, he interpreted to them the things about himself in all the scriptures" (Luke 24:25–27).

That Jesus fulfills the words of the prophets, that is, gives the words of the prophets a fuller meaning, is a theme in Matthew's gospel. In his sermon on the mount, Jesus says, "Do not think that I have come to abolish the law or the prophets; I have come not to abolish but to fulfill" (Matt 5:17). That events are fulfilling the words of the prophets becomes a refrain in Matthew. For instance, when Jesus is arrested, Matthew pictures Jesus saying: "Have you come out with swords and clubs to arrest me as though I were a bandit? Day after day I sat in the temple teaching, and you did not arrest me. But all this has taken place, so that the scriptures of the prophets may be fulfilled" (Matt 26:55–56).

In fact, the church now understands the whole overarching narrative of the books in the Bible to be one story, the story of God's plan for the whole human race. As the *Catechism of the Catholic Church* says, we are to "[b]e especially attentive 'to the content and unity of the whole Scripture.' Different as the books which comprise it may be, Scripture is a unity by reason of the unity of God's plan, of which Christ Jesus is the center and heart, open since his Passover" (no. 112).

PERSONAL GUIDANCE

A second way in which Scripture is a living word is that it can give spiritual insight to each of us individually in the context of our personal lives. We can be reading Scripture, and the words seem to be speaking directly to us: encouraging us, correcting us, and guiding us. The meaning we derive from Scripture when it becomes a living word in the context of our personal lives is not necessarily the meaning that the original author was expressing.

Jesus is pictured as hearing Scripture in this way himself. In Luke's gospel, when Jesus goes to the synagogue in his hometown, Nazareth, he reads from the scroll of Isaiah. Luke tells us that Jesus "unrolled the scroll and found the place where it was written: 'The Spirit of the Lord is upon me,/because he has anointed me/to bring good news to the poor./He has sent me to proclaim release to the captives/and recovery of sight to the blind,/to let the oppressed go free,/to proclaim the year of the Lord's favor'" (Luke 4:17–19).

In the Book of Isaiah, the prophet is not prognosticating Jesus' ministry through these words. Rather, he is describing his own call and mission (see Is 61:1–3). However, in Scripture, the words became living words. Jesus found that the words also described his understanding of his own call and mission. So, after rolling up the scroll, Jesus says, "'Today this scripture has been fulfilled in your hearing.' All spoke well of him and were amazed at the gracious words that came from his mouth" (Luke 4:22).

Just as Scripture was a living word for Jesus, so can it be for us. It is not at all unusual for people who integrate Scripture into their prayer lives to have certain words grab their attention, take hold of their minds, and replay themselves in their memories. The words are experienced as God speaking directly to their hearts. Often when I am teaching that Scripture is a living word, I ask those in the class if they have experienced Scripture in this way. Invariably, several hands go up.

I have, on occasion, had this experience myself. When I have heard Scripture as a living word, the passage has often expressed praise and gratitude, such as, "The Mighty One has done great things for me,/and holy is his name" (Luke 1:49). On other occasions, the words have been correcting me, calling me to be less judgmental and more loving, such as, "Who are you to pass judgment on servants of another?" (Rom 14:4). The words have never told me what is wrong with someone else.

SCRIPTURE AS A LIVING WORD IN THE LITURGY

A third way in which Scripture is a living word is illustrated by the way in which the Catholic Church integrates Scripture into our liturgical life. As explained in Chapter 1, at Mass we proclaim readings from both the Old and New Testaments. In addition, biblical passages are included in every celebration of the sacraments. Scripture is core to the Liturgy of the Hours, the official daily prayer of the church. As a church, we never gather for worship or celebration without hearing Scripture.

Also, when welcoming new members into the Catholic Church, we teach candidates (people who are already baptized) and catechumens (people who are not yet baptized) to *break open the word,* that is, to hear a particular Sunday's readings in the context of the life of the community and in the context of their own lives.

Sometimes we, the church, are listening to the word, seeking understanding and insight from it. Other times, we are praying the word, as we do with the psalms, and the word becomes our own prayer, just as surely as it was the prayer of the Israelites in the second temple.

In integrating Scripture as a living word into our liturgies and into our prayer lives, we are doing just what we are admonished to do in Colossians: "Let the word of Christ dwell in you richly; teach and admonish one another in all wisdom; and with gratitude in your hearts sing psalms, hymns, and spiritual songs to God" (Col 3:16).

HEARING THE LIVING WORD AS CONTEXTUALISTS

When we began this chapter we claimed that even though Scripture is a living word that can speak to us in the contexts of our own community and individual lives, it is still absolutely essential to be a contextualist, to understand what the original inspired authors intended to teach. Why? Because, although Scripture as a living word can say something in addition to what the original inspired authors were teaching, Scripture, when correctly heard as a living word, cannot contradict what the inspired authors were teaching. Therefore, when hearing Scripture as a living word, we need to know what the inspired authors were teaching, in order to determine whether or not the meaning we are hearing in the words is compatible with the overall message of Scripture.

An example I have often used to illustrate this necessity when teaching catechists how to facilitate a group that is *breaking open the word* is the following: How would you respond to a person who says, "I am going to become a suicide bomber because there is no greater love than to lay down your life for your friend" (see John 15:13)? Obviously, what the individual has heard the words saying in the context of his or her life can't be from the Holy Spirit because it contradicts the overall message of Scripture. In such a situation, the catechist needs to know the overall message of Scripture as well as the intent of the author who wrote these words, in order to explain that this interpretation of Scripture as a living word is in error.

If we don't know how to interpret Scripture in context, we have no way of knowing whether what we hear Scripture saying as a living word is compatible with what the inspired authors are teaching. Sadly, history has taught us this lesson over and over. In our next chapter, *The Use and Abuse of Scripture*, we will explore this topic further.

❈ *Questions for Reflection or Discussion*

1. When you look back on your life, do you see meaning in events that you didn't see when the events were occurring? Do you think God has a plan for you? Do you think God has a plan for the whole human race? Explain your responses.

2. What passages in Scripture have helped you name and understand an experience you have had, whether the experience was one of joy, of suffering, of awe, of being saved, etc.?

3. Has Scripture been a living word in your life, correcting, encouraging, and guiding you? Explain your response.

4. Have you ever heard people abuse Scripture to support their own prejudices? Do you feel equipped to explain why this is an abuse of Scripture? What might you do to become prepared?

The Use *and* Abuse
of Scripture

In previous chapters, we have discussed the fact that the Catholic Church teaches us to be contextualists and to put the authority of Scripture behind the intent of the inspired authors. At the same time, we have insisted that Scripture is a living word that can correct and guide us personally and that can cut to the marrow of the bone. We have also seen that the living words of Scripture can mean more than the original human authors intended, in that Old Testament passages are discovered to have an additional level of meaning in the light of Christ's passion, death, and resurrection. The fact that all of these truths need to be held in tension with each other raises the question: What is use and what is abuse of Scripture?

As we will soon illustrate, history has taught us the absolute importance of asking and answering this question. If we ignore the problem, we put ourselves in jeopardy of inadvertently teaching error in God's name and/or inadvertently persecuting innocent people.

When I am teaching the importance of addressing this question, I always use historic examples rather than contemporary examples. The reason for this is that I am trying to teach a method of correctly understanding and hearing Scripture. If I pick a contemporary example, I may trigger a very defensive reaction in people who do not agree with me on the contemporary issue.

I am not met with this resistance when I use examples on which we have now reached agreement, such as the fact that the sun, not the earth, is the center of the movement of the planets, that it is beneath the dignity of a person who has been created in God's own image to be the property of another, and that women should have the right to vote. Once a person has understood the importance of asking the question as to whether or not Scripture is being abused and has learned a method to answer that question, he or she will be able to apply the same method to contemporary issues.

While the issues named are settled for us, they were very contentious topics in previous centuries. As we will see, well-meaning people used Scripture to argue that the earth is the center of the movement of the planets, that slavery as it was practiced in the United States is moral, and that women should not be allowed to vote. In other words, they tried to give authority to their opinions, to argue that God was on their side, by using Scripture to "proof-text" topics that the inspired biblical authors were not addressing in the first place. If we examine just where these well-meaning people went wrong, there is every hope that we can avoid making the same mistakes ourselves.

GALILEO

When Galileo agreed with Copernicus that the sun, not the earth, is the center of the movement of the planets, church authorities silenced him, put him under house arrest, and made him endure the Inquisition. Why? Because Galileo's accusers claimed that his theory that the earth moves around the sun contradicts Scripture. A passage from Scripture that was used to prove that the earth is stable and does not move was taken from Psalm 96:10: "The world is firmly established; it shall never be moved." The same passage appears in 1 Chronicles 16:30: "The world is firmly established; it shall never be moved." Both the passage from Psalms and the passage from 1 Chronicles reflect a presumption of the time of the author and audience: that the earth rests on pillars; it is stable and does not move. However, the inspired authors are not teaching anything about the movement of the planets. They are simply describing God's creation as they presume it is.

The question the authors are addressing is one that is relevant to our spiritual lives. To discover what the authors are teaching, we need only put the passage in the context in which it appears in the Bible. Both Psalm 96 and 1 Chronicles are teaching that God is a great king who will come to judge the world. Psalm 96 says: "Say among the nations, 'The Lord is king!/The world is firmly established; it shall never be moved./ He will judge the peoples with equity'" (Ps 96:10). The firmness of the earth is mentioned as one of God's marvelous creations.

The psalm goes on to call on all of creation to praise this powerful and just God: "Let the heavens be glad, and let the earth rejoice;/let the sea roar, and all that fills it;/let the field exult, and everything in it./Then shall all the trees of the forest sing for joy/ before the Lord; for he is coming,/for he is coming to judge the earth./He will judge the world with righteousness,/and the peoples with his truth" (Ps 96:11–13).

Galileo was not contradicting Scripture by proposing his theory, because no biblical author ever addressed the question of the movement of the planets. Biblical authors are not teaching science, so we cannot use out-of-context passages of Scripture to argue for or against any scientific theory.

Because church authorities, over time, came to this understanding, Pope (now Saint) John Paul II formally apologized for the way in which Galileo had been treated. Speaking to the Pontifical Academy of Sciences in 1992, he also named with great precision just what had caused the problem: "The majority of theologians did not recognize the formal distinction between Sacred Scripture and its interpretation, and this led them unduly to transpose into the realm of the doctrine of the faith a question which in fact pertained to scientific investigation."

Pope John Paul II warned theologians not to repeat the mistake that church authorities made with Galileo. When speaking of the necessity for theologians not to try to speak with authority on scientific matters, the pope said, "The birth of a new way of approaching study of natural phenomena demands a clarification on the part of all disciplines of knowledge. It obliges them to define more clearly their own field, their approach, their methods, as well as the precise import of the conclusions. In other words, this new way requires each discipline to become more rigorously aware of its own nature."

Since no biblical author is addressing a scientific question, whenever the Bible is used to argue either for or against a scientific theory, the Bible is being abused. The Bible does not speak with authority on any scientific question. When a statement is made that appears to address a scientific topic, that statement is an example of the beliefs and presumptions of the author and his audience.

SLAVERY

Another example from history of the abuse of Scripture is the way Scripture was used in the United States only one hundred fifty years ago when the country was arguing about the morality of slavery. Those who supported slavery as it was practiced in the United States quoted the letter to the Ephesians: "Slaves, obey your earthly masters with fear and trembling, in singleness of heart, as you obey Christ; not only while being watched, and in order to please them, but as slaves of Christ, doing the will of God from the heart" (Eph 6:5–6).

Slavery's supporters quoted this passage to argue that slavery was part of God's social order. They never asked themselves: Is the author of this passage addressing the question I am using the passage to address—the question of the morality of slavery? If they had asked themselves this question, they would not have used the passage as they did.

The author of Ephesians is teaching a core truth of Christianity: "Therefore be imitators of God, as beloved children, and live in love, as Christ loved us and gave himself up for us, a fragrant offering and sacrifice to God" (Eph 5:1–2). He then applies this insight to the social order of the people to whom he is writing his letter (the literary form). In this social order, slaves and wives were property. The author does not ask if they should be. They are.

Given that social order, the author instructs masters, slaves, husbands, wives, parents, children—those in authority and those under authority—to act in love toward others. The author is applying a core truth to a particular social setting. He is teaching people how to love one another, given the social situation in which they are living. He is not teaching that slavery is part of God's social order.

A core message of Scripture that affects the way in which we organize our society is that God is love and that we must love one another as people of great dignity, created in the image of God. This core message can be applied to any number of social orders. No biblical author is endorsing one social order over another. However, every social order should be judged according to this core teaching. A social order that allows one person to be the property of another is not honoring the dignity of the person who is owned, a person who is a beloved child of God. To use Scripture to support a social order that enslaves others is to abuse Scripture.

WOMEN SUFFRAGE

Even closer to our time in history, the Bible was used to argue against allowing women to vote in the United States. It was not until 1920 that the nineteenth amendment to the Constitution affirmed that the right to vote could not be denied a person on the basis of his or her sex. Among the passages used to try to deny women the vote were two passages from the story we used in Chapter 3 as our example of applying the contextualist method of interpretation to an Old Testament text: the story of the man and woman in the garden.

Those who were against women suffrage quoted two passages from this story: The first is the passage in which God is pictured as saying, "It is not good that the man should be alone; I will make him a helper as his partner" (Gen 2:18). The second is when God explains to the woman the ramifications of the man and woman's having eaten from the tree of the knowledge of good and evil: "Your desire will be for your husband, and he shall rule over you" (Gen 3:16b).

Based on these passages, people used Scripture to put God's authority behind their prejudices and to marginalize women who, like men, are made in the image of God. The argument was that the first passage proved that women were created to be men's helpmates. The second passage was used to argue that it is part of God's social order that husbands have authority over their wives. Therefore, women's role was limited to domestic affairs. She had no role in public affairs. Women should not be allowed to vote.

As we explained in Chapter 3, the story of the man and

woman in the garden is addressing the question of why human beings suffer. While the story does not provide us with a total answer to that question, it does teach us something that is universally true: sin causes suffering. The story is not addressing the question that was being asked in the early twentieth century: Should women have the right to vote in a democratic society? To use out-of-context passages from the story to address an entirely different question is to abuse, not use, Scripture.

What conclusions are we to draw from these historical examples? Scripture is a living word, so we do want to listen to what this living word has to say as we discern proper action in twenty-first-century settings. However, we are abusing Scripture, rather than listening to the living word, when we take out-of-context biblical passages to proof-text conclusions on subjects that the original inspired authors were not addressing.

From the examples given, we can conclude that no inspired biblical author ever addressed a scientific question. In addition, no inspired biblical author mandated a specific social order. As we explained in Chapter 1, the biblical authors were addressing a different topic: Who is God? Who are we in relationship to God? How would God have us act so as to cooperate with the coming of God's kingdom rather than to thwart it? As the Catholic Church teaches us, bottom line, the topic is: What do we need to know for the sake of our salvation?

For the sake of our salvation, we do not need to know the shape of the earth, or the movement of the planets, or the number of years it took life forms to appear on the earth. What we do need to know is that God is love, that human beings, male and female, are created in God's image and so are people of great and equal dignity, and that no matter in what social order we live, we are required to apply the core truths of Scripture, love of God and love of neighbor, to the setting in which we find ourselves.

How can we avoid the mistakes of the past when addressing present-day social issues? No matter how well-meaning, we do not want to abuse Scripture passages by using them to argue that God ordained what are actually our own prejudices and practices. In order to avoid perpetuating this mistake in the future, we must take to heart what St. John Paul II said: we must make a clear distinction between what Scripture actually says and how we have interpreted what Scripture says. If the passage we are using to proof-text our own position has nothing to do with what the inspired biblical author was using the words to say, we are abusing Scripture when we quote it to support our point of view. To avoid this mistake, we need only ask ourselves: Is the topic I am using these words to address the same topic that the inspired biblical author is addressing? If the answer is no, then we should not use the out-of-context words to claim that the authority of Scripture, and, therefore, God, is on our side of the argument.

⊛ *Questions for Reflection or Discussion*

1. Have you ever heard people who are on opposite sides of an issue both use Scripture to support their points of view? How is this possible? What does such a situation tell you about the importance of being a contextualist?

---

2. Have you ever heard anyone use Scripture to proof-text his or her own opinion on a contemporary scientific theory or on a current social issue? What was the issue? What were the arguments? Was the person using or abusing Scripture?

---

3. Have you ever used Scripture to proof-text your opinion on a contemporary scientific or social issue? Based on what you know now, in doing this were you using or abusing Scripture?

---

4. Why is proof-texting so dangerous? What questions do we need to ask ourselves in order to make sure that we are using, not abusing, Scripture?

A Reflection *on* Age-Appropriate Catechesis

In the previous chapters, we have been responding to the question: What do adult catechists need to know about Scripture in order to teach Scripture to any age group? In addressing this question, we have consistently cautioned that not everything catechists need to know is appropriate content to teach their students. In this chapter we will discuss the fact that people understand religious concepts differently, depending on their age. Catechists need to be particularly aware of two important stages in children's cognitive development.

Age-appropriate catechesis is a very important topic. After all, the goals of our religious education programs include not just passing on information, but forming disciples of Jesus Christ who understand the good news of the gospel and who strive to apply that good news to their own daily lives. Knowledge is certainly a desired outcome, but so are faith, joy, hope, peace, and love. The reason knowledge of age-appropriate catechesis is important is that if we teach something not suitable for the age of our students, we may plant doubt rather than faith. We may plant confusion rather than peace. We may plant discouragement rather than hope. We may plant resistance rather than love.

Because I now have over fifty years' experience as a catechist, I can address this topic by reflecting on my own experience. As I think about my years of teaching, I recall two events that occurred before I learned what will be explained in this chapter: that each of us undergoes a process of cognitive development as we grow older, and for this reason we understand concepts differently depending on our age and experience. It is important that catechists realize that children think and understand things differently than do adults. If we forget this, we are in danger of correcting a child's understanding by explaining our own in an age-inappropriate way.

When I was a college student in 1961, I volunteered to teach a first-grade CCD class in a nearby parish. As a twenty-year-old beginning catechist, I did not know what I am soon going to explain about the way children think. I was the youngest child in my own family, and I had had very little interaction with people younger than myself. I didn't give sufficient thought to the differences between what I myself was just beginning to understand as an adult and what a child is capable of understanding.

I particularly remember Passion Sunday when I was explaining, in as simple language as I could muster, just what Jesus Christ had accomplished for all of us through his passion, death, and resurrection. After a too-lengthy explanation, I stopped and asked, "Do you have any questions?" There was dead silence. Finally, one little boy, who, to this day, I think was feeling sorry for me and trying to help me out of this awkward situation, raised his hand. "Yes, John?" I said. He, full of enthusiasm, said, "I have a pet gerbil."

Obviously, my message, though central to the liturgical year and core to the good news of the gospel, was not delivered in an age-appropriate way. Perhaps, instead of starting with the passion, death, and resurrection, I could have started with some Easter eggs. I could have asked if they were going to have an Easter egg hunt. I could have asked what they know about eggs: Have they ever seen a chicken peck its way out of an egg? I could have explained in a very literal way that new life comes from eggs. The reason we have eggs at Easter is that Easter is a celebration of new life too. We know about our new life because of Jesus and his resurrection. The passion and death need not have taken central stage, even though what I had said was true to Passion Sunday and to our tradition. It simply wasn't age appropriate. My students taught me that.

A second event occurred fourteen years later, in 1975. By this time I was married, had four little children, and was teaching two classes on Scripture at our local Catholic high school. My students were seniors. I taught them the contextualist approach to Scripture, just as I have explained it in earlier chapters. Most of the students loved the class. They were like sponges soaking it all up. I felt just wonderful about their eagerness to learn and their understanding.

However, the administration decided to change the curriculum and to have a course on marriage offered to the seniors. So, the course I was teaching on Scripture was moved to the sophomore level. I taught the sophomores just what I had taught with such success to the seniors. The outcome was drastically different. When taught that the literary form of a particular story was not history, the students went home and told their parents that I had taught them that "the Bible is not true." Most of the sophomores did not understand that symbols are not literal facts or that we use metaphorical language when talking about God (to be explained soon).

Neither the principal, the head of the religion department,

nor I understood why the seniors had understood what was being taught and found it wonderfully exhilarating and faith building, while the sophomores had not. The book that explained this to me, *Stages of Faith: The Psychology of Human Development and the Quest for Meaning,* by James W. Fowler, was not published until 1981. Fowler, building on the work of Piaget (cognitive development) and Kohlberg (moral development), taught me two facts about the relationship between cognitive and faith development that enabled me to understand the reasons behind what I knew to be true from experience.

AGE THREE TO SEVEN

Children between the age of three and seven are in the process of learning how to distinguish between what is real and what is imaginative. I had a conversation with one of my grandchildren that perfectly illustrated this stage of cognitive development. As we began a walk around our neighborhood, she said to me: "OK. You are not my grandma. You are not my mom. You are my fairy godmother." So, that statement was the context for the whole walk. She was constantly including me, her fairy godmother, in what was going on in her imagination.

We live in Lexington, Kentucky, near Henry Clay's home. The property includes a carriage house with the carriage Henry Clay used to travel to Washington, DC. As we were walking around the property my granddaughter asked, "Are you related to Henry Clay?" Thinking I was continuing our game, I said, "I'm related to him the same way I am related to you. I was his fairy godmother." Then I showed her the carriage that Henry Clay's fairy godmother (like Cinderella's fairy godmother) had given him for his trip to Washington, DC. She looked at me with wonder and then skepticism and said, "You're kidding, aren't you?" When she saw me smiling at her, full of amusement, she laughed and said, "You *are* kidding." She was expertly working out exactly the cognitive challenge of her age group: what is real and what is imaginary. This grandchild represents the thinking of many, if not most, of the children who will be in a second-grade first communion class.

This conversation reminded me of a comment one of my own children made when he was about the same age. He told me that he didn't know if he wanted to be an astronaut or a priest. The problem with being a priest was that he wasn't sure he could "work that trick." I asked, "What trick?" He said, "The trick where the priest turns the bread and wine into the body and blood of Christ."

Thomas Aquinas tried to explain the mystery of Christ's true presence in the Eucharist by using Greek philosophical categories of thought, such as *transubstantiation*. No second grader can understand that abstract concept. The cognitive development of a second grader, who is still trying to discern the difference between that which is real and that which is imaginary, is much more likely to think in terms of magic. Still, second graders do understand the concept being taught, that Christ is truly present in Eucharist.

AGE EIGHT TO FIFTEEN

Children between the age of eight and fifteen understand images literally. They understand the meaning that an image conveys, but they also think that the image is a matter of fact, not a metaphor. I was extremely interested in learning this because it explained why nearly all the seniors (seventeen years old) whom I had taught to be contextualists understood everything I taught, and almost none of the sophomores (fifteen years old) were able to understand the same concepts.

Fowler explains that once young people have sorted out what is real and what is not real, they are very literal in their thinking. They understand the meaning that an image conveys, but they take the image literally and are unable to separate the image from the meaning behind it. Nearly all adults are capable of moving beyond this literal stage in cognitive development, but many fail to do so. If a person's religious education ends with confirmation (perhaps in eighth or ninth grade), that person is likely to continue to understand the symbolic language we use to name religious concepts as statements of fact, not as metaphors to probe mystery.

Once I learned about this stage of cognitive and faith development from reading Fowler's book, I tested it out by visiting an eighth-grade class. I asked the class, "What does it mean to say that God holds you in the palm of God's hand?" Every child in the class knew what truth was being taught through that metaphor. They all agreed that it means that God lovingly takes care of us.

I then asked, "Does God have hands?" The students looked at me as though I had lost my mind. Why would I ask such a ridiculous question? They all knew that God has hands. However, the question upset one eighth-grade boy. He leapt out of his desk. He pounded his fist on the top of his desk. He looked me straight in the eye and said, "Of course God has hands. If God didn't have hands, God couldn't hold us in the palm of his hands."

Later the teacher told me that the boy who said this was the brightest boy in the class. He was still understanding the metaphor "hand" literally, but he was beginning to comprehend that maybe God didn't have hands. That was a very scary thought, because if God didn't have hands, how could we be in God's hands? This anxiety was the source of his adamancy. He was just beginning the task of growing into adulthood in his faith. He was beginning to be able to separate the symbol, hand, from the meaning behind the symbol, God's providential care. Most of us do not develop the ability to do this until we are juniors or seniors in high school.

The seniors who loved learning how to be contextualists had the cognitive ability to understand that a story like the man and woman in the garden is not teaching science or history, but it is teaching truth. Most of the sophomores did not. For them, if the story was not scientifically and historically factual, it was not true. Both ages were able to understand what the story was teaching: that sin causes suffering. But only the seniors were able to understand the symbols as vehicles for truth even though they were not naming historical or scientific facts.

To be able to understand the way symbolic language functions as we think and speak about spiritual realities is most welcome to adults. If Catholics were not biblical contextualists, we would mistakenly think that a great deal of what we learn from other areas of knowledge is contradictory to Scripture. It is because Catholics are contextualists that we find the idea of evolution and the creation stories in the Bible to be compatible with each other.

As catechists we must have an adult understanding of Scripture ourselves, but we must also meet our students where they are. We must do our best to explain things in language that they can understand and, at the same time, not say anything that, when they get just a little older, they will realize is not true. We will discuss some ideas on how to accomplish this most important goal in our next chapter on catechetical methods.

⬤ Questions for Reflection or Discussion

1. Do you have any memory of having imaginary friends? or of fearing monsters under the bed? Have you had conversations with children in which they have included you in their imaginative perceptions of reality? Explain. How do you think a child of six or seven imagines God? How do you think experience would influence this image of God?

2. When you think back on your own spiritual development, do you remember understanding religious concepts more literally than you understand them now? For instance, what was your concept of God? of heaven? of guardian angels? Has your understanding of these realities changed with age?

3. How would a typical senior in high school and a typical eighth grader differ in their understanding of the story of Adam and Eve? Why might it be harmful to teach an adult understanding of this story to an eighth grader?

4. What does it mean to say that children understand the message conveyed by metaphorical language, but they understand the metaphor to be literally true? Can you give any examples? Why is it important for an adult to outgrow this stage of cognitive development? What difficulties with religious beliefs might an adult have after taking a science course if he or she does not grow beyond this literal understanding?

A Reflection *on* Catechetical Methods

When I reflect on my years of being a catechist—as a parent, a grandparent, and a parish and diocesan catechist teaching various age groups (kindergarteners, eighth graders, high school sophomores, juniors, and seniors, and adults in adult education groups and catechist certification programs)—I can reflect on both what I did right and what I did wrong. I described two of the things I did wrong in our last chapter, on age-appropriate catechesis. In this chapter I would like to reflect on what, from experience, I know works. What are common elements of good catechesis when teaching Scripture, no matter the age of the students?

BE A LIFELONG LEARNER

When I was twenty years old, and I volunteered to be a parish catechist, I had a great deal to learn myself. A twenty-year-old is still growing into adult faith. However, now, at seventy-four, I can make exactly the same statement: I still have a great deal to learn. I am still growing in my faith and in my understanding in the light of new knowledge.

Good catechists are lifelong learners, not finished products. This is particularly true of a catechist who teaches Scripture. We could study Scripture our whole lives and still have more to learn. We learn from being in conversation with our students. We learn from being in conversation with other catechists. We learn from the textbooks, teacher manuals, and online resources provided by Catholic publishers and approved by our parish or diocese. We learn from catechist certification programs. We learn from experience. If we wait to become catechists until after we know everything that would be helpful to know, we will never become catechists.

MODEL CHRIST'S LOVE

As catechists, especially catechists who teach Scripture, we are echoing the good news of the gospel. The core good news centers around Jesus Christ and what has been revealed through Christ's teachings, passion, death, and resurrection. Jesus taught that the whole law and the prophets can be summed up in two commandments: love of God and love of neighbor (see Matt 22:36–40). The core of the good news of Scripture is the priority of love.

When we teach, we teach not only by what we say, but by how we act. It is of absolute importance that our whole demeanor, our every action, be a faithful witness of God's love for God's people. The more loving we can be, the more credible and attractive will be our teaching. The more loving we are, the more our students will be able to believe that God is love (see 1 John 4:7–8).

BEGIN EVERY CLASS WITH PRAYER

In addition to modeling God's love, catechists must model a life of prayer. No matter how young our students are, and no matter their stage in cognitive and faith development, they are capable of having a deep spiritual life. Prayer might involve naming those things for which we want to thank God and inviting the students to do the same. It might involve asking God for help with special challenges and inviting the students to do the same. Prayers from Scripture could be included: psalms of thanksgiving and hymns of praise. The teacher need not always lead the prayer. Students can be invited to compose prayers and lead the class in thanking and praising God.

KNOW YOUR STUDENTS

We have already discussed the importance of knowing something about the way students understand religious concepts, depending on their age. In addition, students bring many other experiences with them that shape their image of God, as well as their ability to understand any other concept that we are trying to teach. In order to know our students, we must engage them in dialogue, we must invite questions, and we must know something about their culture—what they watch on TV and what games they play. This knowledge will help us to word things in a way that will have some relevance to their experience and that will be more understandable to them.

I witnessed a perfect example of this when listening to a mother and her six-year-old son describe a harrowing experience. A car had backed into the child, and actually run over him, but he didn't have so much as a broken bone. The mother and child both experienced the event as one in which God was powerful and present. The mother couldn't think of anything to say other than to exclaim, "It was a miracle! It was a miracle!" When asked if he thought what had happened to him was a miracle, the child said, "Well, I don't know about that. I think God turned me into SpongeBob." The child didn't know what the word *miracle* meant, but he was perfectly capable of explaining his experience in a way that his peers would understand.

By engaging students in dialogue, catechists learn more and more about the children's life circumstances and their way of expressing themselves in the light of their own knowledge and experiences. The more we know about our students, the better catechists we become.

SCRIPTURE IN THE CHILD'S EXPERIENCE

In a Catholic setting, Scripture is part of a child's experience at every level of cognitive development. Children, no matter their age, are present at Sunday Mass and hear that week's Scripture passages proclaimed from the Lectionary. The priest or deacon gives a homily based on the readings. Usually, the homily is directed primarily at the adults in the congregation. Given what we now know about cognitive and faith development, the children's understanding of what they have heard and their parents' understanding will be quite different. Catechists of every age group must have an adult understanding of the readings and be prepared to respond in an age-appropriate manner to any questions that might come up.

In addition to hearing Scripture passages at Mass, Catholic children become acquainted with some passages of Scripture because they are integrated into the textbooks used for children's religious education. During the early stages of cognitive development, Scripture itself is not being taught: textbooks do not explain the literary form of the passage, the presumptions of the author and audience, or where this particular insight fits into the two-thousand-year process of revelation that is present in Scripture. Rather, Scripture is used as a means of teaching doctrine and morals. The students don't read the Bible; they read an account of a biblical story that is retold in an age-appropriate way.

For instance, the author of one first-grade textbook, in retelling the story of Adam and Eve, says, "But one day, the devil pretended he was a snake and came into the garden. He told Eve to go ahead and try some of the forbidden fruit from the tree. He said it would make her just as smart as God."[1] A catechist with an adult understanding of the story knows that the idea that "the devil pretended he was a snake" is the author's attempt to translate the meaning of a symbol (the talking snake symbolizes temptation, an abstract concept that a first grader cannot understand) in a way that a first grader can understand: imagining or pretending to be someone else (like a fairy godmother).

The lesson goes on to teach what is meant by the word *sin,* and that bad things happen when we sin. First graders can understand that if they disobey God, their parents, or their teachers, something bad will happen. What the students are learning about sin and its consequences is true. At the same time, the students will think the story is describing reality, that it is describing events just as they occurred. As they develop cognitively, they will realize that this understanding is not accurate.

In contrast, a textbook for ages twelve to fifteen, in referring to the same story to teach why the human race needed to be redeemed, says, "This story uses figurative language to make its point. The sin of Adam and Eve wasn't eating a piece of fruit. It was their decision to live a life separate from God. God didn't punish them; they punished themselves by the choice they made. It's no surprise that they discovered that a life without God was not a happy life."[2]

---

1   "Our Heavenly Father," Faith and Life Series, Third Edition, Book One (Ignatius Press, San Francisco, 2011) p. 27.

2   Joe Paprocki, "Called to Be Catholic: Essentials of the Catholic Faith for Ages 12-15" (Loyola Press, Chicago, 2014) p. 19.

Here the author is just beginning to explain that the story, while it teaches something true, is using symbolic language to teach truth, not literally describing an event. However, the author does not apply the concept of literary form to the story. That would be age inappropriate. The students would misunderstand the author to be saying that the story, and, therefore, the Bible, is not true (remember my experience when teaching this to sophomores in high school).

This textbook also draws the students' attention to the Bible in its own right. When explaining that Scripture and Tradition are two forms of God's revelation, the author says, "The Bible, the sacred book of the Christian faith, is composed of 73 books of different types."[3] However, one must wait a few more years to explain exactly what is meant by "books of different types." Most students can't begin to understand and appreciate the ramifications of the fact that the Bible is a library of books of different literary forms until they are at least seventeen.

SCRIPTURE IN THE CURRICULUM

If the Bible in its own right is not the object of study in the early grades, should Bible stories be used to teach doctrine and morals? I think there is no better way to teach doctrine and morals than through biblical stories. Not only are the children becoming acquainted with the stories—knowledge that will be the foundation for what they will be able to understand later—but the children realize that what is true for the people in the stories is true for them: Sin leads to suffering in their lives too. God loves and forgives them too. God wants them to live in God's love and to love each other. It is because people of all ages can learn moral lessons from stories that telling stories,

---

3   Ibid. p. 5

telling parables, was Jesus' primary method of teaching.

Learning to understand Scripture, to understand what eternal truths about our salvation the inspired authors are teaching, is a lifetime endeavor, both for ourselves and for our students. As we grow in our own knowledge, and as we do our best to share our knowledge in an age-appropriate way with others, we will be helping Christ's body, the church, become who we are called to be, a people nourished and ruled by Scripture.

❁ *Questions for Reflection or Discussion*

1. What opportunities do you have to grow in your knowledge and faith? What concrete steps are you taking to be a lifelong learner?

---

2. Why does your whole demeanor affect your ability to be an effective witness of the good news of the gospel?

---

3. Why do you think discussion about stories, especially Bible stories, is such an effective way to teach doctrinal and moral truths, no matter the age of the students?

---

4. How long have you been a catechist? When you reflect on your own experience, what have you learned about what works and what doesn't work?

Conclusion

Recently when I was teaching a group of adults how to be biblical contextualists, a man raised his hand and, with some impatience in his voice, said, "The Bible is the Bible. It can speak for itself. Don't you think you are making this more complicated than it has to be?" He was hearing information he had not previously been taught, and he was feeling resistant. I tried my best to explain to this person why I think that all Christian adults would greatly benefit from understanding the contextualist approach, the Catholic approach, to Scripture.

When the same question is asked in relation to adults who are teaching Scripture, I believe that it is absolutely necessary that catechists be well-informed contextualists, no matter the age of the students the catechists are teaching. Students who are learning about Scripture need a teacher who understands the Bible as an adult in order to engage not only the students, but, perhaps, the students' parents, in dialogue. Remember, the parents themselves may not have developed beyond the literal stage of thinking.

As catechists who teach Scripture, we have to be able to explain how the Catholic Church can treasure a story in which all that exists is created in six days (Gen 1:1—2:4) and, at the same time, accept the idea of evolution (consider literary form). We have to be able to explain why, although Scripture says that slaves should obey their masters (Eph 6:5), the Catholic Church teaches against slavery (consider the beliefs of the time). We have to be able to explain why, although Scripture says "you shall give life for life, eye for eye, tooth for tooth..." (Ex 21:23–24), the Catholic Church teaches against the death penalty (consider the process of revelation).

However, being contextualists is not the be-all and end-all of our understanding of Scripture. We must also help others hear Scripture as a living word for the church as a whole (the Lectionary) as well as a living word in the lives of individuals (a person's prayer life). When people share with us what they have heard this living word say, we must know the overall message of Scripture so that we can help them discern whether the meaning they are deriving from Scripture is truly of the Spirit or if it is an example of proof-texting, of taking a passage of Scripture out of context and using it to support a deep-seated prejudice.

Scripture is one of the greatest gifts that the church has received. Scripture truly does teach us what we need to know for our salvation. As catechists who teach Scripture, let us be faithful witnesses of the good news that we have been privileged to receive.